GIANT-O-SAURS

by Nancy White

Consultant: Luis M. Chiappe, Ph.D.
Director of the Dinosaur Institute
Natural History Museum of Los Angeles County

BEARPORT
PUBLISHING

NEW YORK, NEW YORK

Credits

Title Page, © Luis Rey; TOC, © Phil Wilson; 4-5, © Luis Rey; 6, © Neil Wigmore/Shutterstock; 7, © Luis Rey; 8, © Luis Rey; 9, © John Bindon; 10L, © Phil Wilson; 10R, © Jose Fuente/Shutterstock; 11, © John Bindon; 12, © ticktock Media Archive; 13, © Highlights For Children/Oxford Scientific/Photolibrary; 14, © Anness Publishing/The Natural History Museum, London; 15, © John Bindon; 16, © The Natural History Museum, London; 17, © 2007 by Karen Carr and Karen Carr Studio, Inc.; 19, © John Sibbick; 20, © Joe Tucciarone/Photo Researchers, Inc.; 21, © Phil Wilson; 23TL, © Anness Publishing/The Natural History Museum, London; 23TR, © Michael C. Gray/Shutterstock; 23BL, © The Natural History Museum, London; 23BR, © Joe Tucciarone/Photo Researchers, Inc.

Publisher: Kenn Goin
Editorial Director: Adam Siegel
Creative Director: Spencer Brinker
Design: Dawn Beard Creative
Cover Illustration: Luis Rey
Photo Researcher: Omni-Photo Communications, Inc.

Library of Congress Cataloging-in-Publication Data

White, Nancy, 1942-
  Giant-o-saurs / by Nancy White.
     p. cm. — (Dino times trivia)
  Includes bibliographical references and index.
  ISBN-13: 978-1-59716-711-6 (library binding)
  ISBN-10: 1-59716-711-8 (library binding)
  1. Dinosaurs—Juvenile literature. I. Title.

  QE861.5.W52 2009
  567.9—dc22

                    2008014392

For more information, write to Bearport Publishing Company, Inc., 101 Fifth Avenue, Suite 6R, New York, New York 10003. Printed in the United States of America in North Mankato, Minnesota.

102010
092110CGC

10 9 8 7 6 5 4 3

Contents

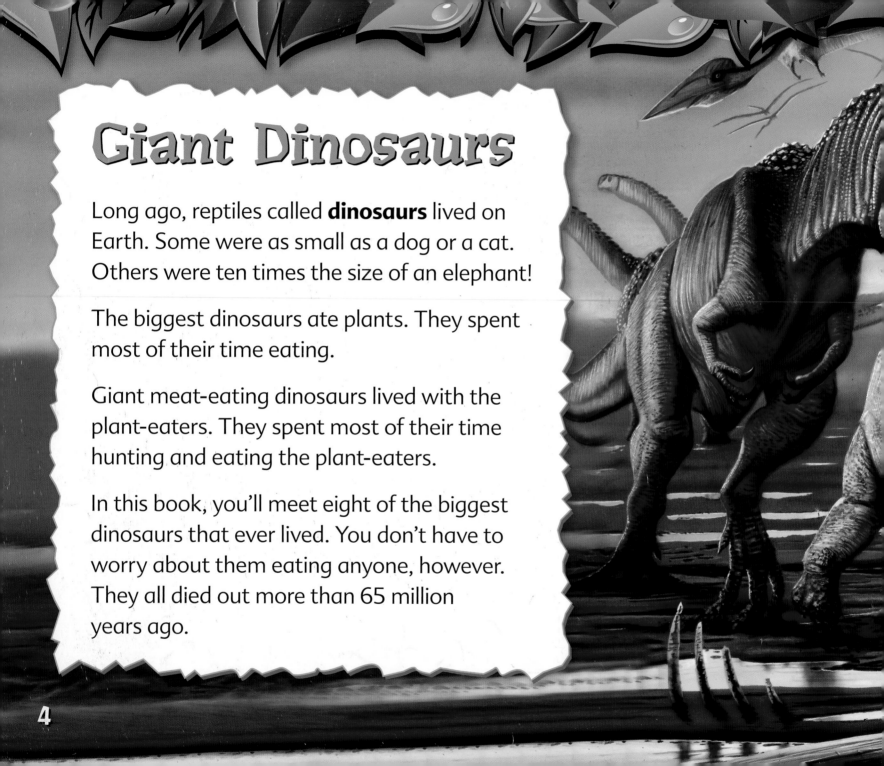

Giant Dinosaurs

Long ago, reptiles called **dinosaurs** lived on Earth. Some were as small as a dog or a cat. Others were ten times the size of an elephant!

The biggest dinosaurs ate plants. They spent most of their time eating.

Giant meat-eating dinosaurs lived with the plant-eaters. They spent most of their time hunting and eating the plant-eaters.

In this book, you'll meet eight of the biggest dinosaurs that ever lived. You don't have to worry about them eating anyone, however. They all died out more than 65 million years ago.

5

Apatosaurus

How big was it?

meters		feet
12 —		— 40
10 —		— 30
8 —		
6 —		— 20
4 —		— 10
2 —		
0		— 0

Apatosaurus was a giant plant-eater. It weighed as much as four elephants.

Apatosaurus may have been too big to walk between some of the trees in a forest. So how did the giant creature get to the leaves it needed to eat?

Apatosaurus could poke its long neck and tiny head into the forest to reach and eat leaves from trees.

elephant

The biggest dinosaurs, such as Apatosaurus, ate only plants. The largest animal living on land today, the elephant, is also a plant-eater.

Diplodocus

How do you say it?
dih-PLOH-duh-kuhss

What does it mean?
double beam

How big was it?

Diplodocus had teeth that were shaped like pegs. They were not sharp enough to bite other animals, however.

How did *Diplodocus* defend itself against giant meat-eaters?

Diplodocus had a long, skinny tail. The giant dinosaur may have lashed its tail like a whip to scare away its enemies.

peg-shaped teeth

8

Diplodocus was as long as three fire engines and weighed as much as two elephants. It was big enough to crush even the biggest meat-eating dinosaurs.

Diplodocus

Allosaurus

Brachiosaurus

How do you say it?
brack-ee-oh-SOR-uhss

What does it mean?
arm reptile

How big was it?

meters		feet
12		40
10		30
8		20
6		
4		10
2		
0		0

Brachiosaurus ate plants. Like many other plant-eating dinosaurs, it also swallowed small stones.

Why did it need to swallow stones?

The small stones that *Brachiosaurus* swallowed went into a special stomach called a gizzard. The stones helped to grind up the plants the dinosaur ate.

Chickens and other birds living today have gizzards. These birds also swallow small stones to help them grind up their food.

Argentinosaurus

How do you say it?
ar-jun-tee-noh-SOR-uhss

What does it mean?
reptile found in Argentina

How big was it?

meters		feet
20		70
15		60
		50
10		40
		30
5		20
		10
0		0

Baby dinosaurs hatched out of eggs, just like chickens. Unlike chickens, however, giant plant-eating dinosaurs were too heavy to sit on their eggs. The shells would have broken.

How did giant dinosaurs like *Argentinosaurus* keep their eggs warm so the babies could hatch?

Scientists think the huge dinosaurs covered their eggs with leaves and branches.

nest of dinosaur eggs

Argentinosaurus is the biggest dinosaur ever found. It was 120 feet (37 m) long—the same length as three school buses parked end to end. It weighed as much as 13 elephants!

Giganotosaurus

How do you say it?
jig-uh-noh-toh-SOR-uhss

What does it mean?
giant southern reptile

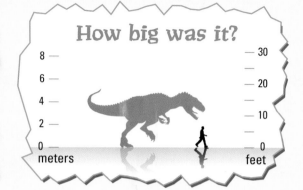

How big was it?

meters		feet
8		30
6		20
4		10
2		
0		0

Giant plant-eating dinosaurs were food for giant meat-eating dinosaurs. *Giganotosaurus* was one of the biggest meat-eaters. It weighed about as much as an elephant. Yet it still wasn't big enough to kill a giant plant-eater by itself.

How did *Giganotosaurus* kill a large plant-eating dinosaur?

Giganotosaurus may have hunted in a pack. The hungry meat-eater could kill a much larger dinosaur when it worked with others in a group.

14

The teeth of *Giganotosaurus* were up to eight inches (20 cm) long. It used them to slice the flesh of large plant-eaters.

Argentinosaurus

Giganotosaurus

Tyrannosaurus rex

How do you say it?
tye-*ran*-uh-SOR-uhss REKS

What does it mean?
tyrant reptile

How big was it?

meters		feet
8		30
6		20
4		10
2		
0		0

Tyrannosaurus rex had about 60 teeth. They were as sharp and long as steak knives. These teeth were so strong they could bite through bone.

What happened if a tooth broke off or fell out?

Another tooth grew back and replaced it.

Tyrannosaurus rex teeth

16

The mouth of Tyrannosaurus rex was so big, a person could climb into it. Its powerful **jaws** could rip off 250 pounds (113 kg) of flesh in one bite.

Allosaurus

How do you say it?
al-oh-SOR-uhss

What does it mean?
strange reptile

How big was it?

Like most giant meat-eaters, *Allosaurus* wasn't very fast. Its top speed was probably around 20 miles per hour (32 kph). Some people can run faster than that.

If *Allosaurus* wasn't very speedy, how was it able to catch and eat giant-plant eaters?

The giant plant-eaters were even slower than *Allosaurus*. They were so big that they probably couldn't run more than 10 miles per hour (16 kph).

19

Spinosaurus

How big was it?

meters | feet

Spinosaurus looked like it had a huge sail attached to its back. The sail was actually a row of long bony **spines** that grew out of the dinosaur's back.

How did the sail keep this meat-eater safe?

The sail made *Spinosaurus* look even bigger than it really was. The extra size might have scared away its enemies.

sail

20

Where Did They Live?

This map shows some of the places where the **fossils** of giant dinosaurs have been found.

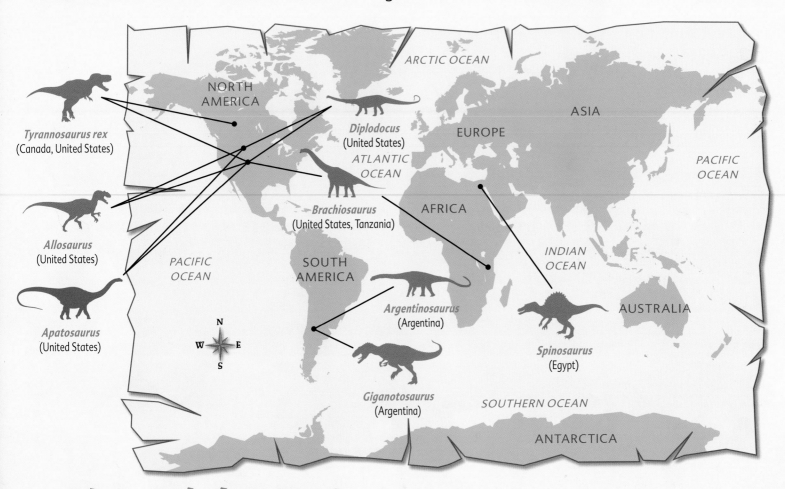

ARCTIC OCEAN

NORTH AMERICA

ASIA

EUROPE

Tyrannosaurus rex
(Canada, United States)

Diplodocus
(United States)

ATLANTIC OCEAN

PACIFIC OCEAN

Allosaurus
(United States)

Brachiosaurus
(United States, Tanzania)

AFRICA

Apatosaurus
(United States)

PACIFIC OCEAN

SOUTH AMERICA

INDIAN OCEAN

N
W   E
S

Argentinosaurus
(Argentina)

AUSTRALIA

Spinosaurus
(Egypt)

Giganotosaurus
(Argentina)

SOUTHERN OCEAN

ANTARCTICA

When Did They Live?

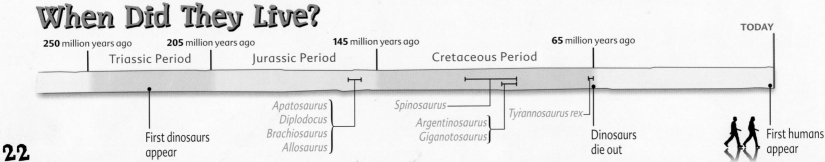

TODAY

250 million years ago   **205** million years ago   **145** million years ago   **65** million years ago

Triassic Period	Jurassic Period	Cretaceous Period

First dinosaurs appear

Apatosaurus
Diplodocus
Brachiosaurus
Allosaurus

Spinosaurus
Argentinosaurus
Giganotosaurus

Tyrannosaurus rex

Dinosaurs die out

First humans appear

Glossary

dinosaurs
(DYE-nuh-sorz)
reptiles that lived
on land more than
65 million years
ago, and then
died out

fossils
(FOSS-uhlz)
what is left of
plants or animals
that lived long ago

jaws
(JAWZ)
bones that
surround an
animal's mouth
and hold its teeth

spines
(SPYENZ)
thin, pointy bones

Index

Read More

Lessem, Don. *Giant Meat-Eating Dinosaurs.* Minneapolis, MN: Lerner Publications (2005).

Lessem, Don. *Giant Plant-Eating Dinosaurs.* Minneapolis, MN: Lerner Publications (2005).

Learn More Online

To learn more about giant dinosaurs, visit
www.bearportpublishing.com/DinoTimesTrivia

About the Author

Nancy White has written many children's books about animals—from butterflies to dinosaurs.